ANGER MANAGEMENT IN THE PRIMARY CLASSROOM
AN INTERVENTION COURSE FOR 7-12 YEAR OLDS

SOCIAL SKILLS

Book Number: K2248
ISDN Number: 1-84321-044-4
Published: 2003

Author
Martin Van Der Kley

Publishers
KCP Publications Ltd.
Woburn House
Wentworth Gardens
Toddington
Bedfordshire
LU5 6DN
United Kingdom
Fax: +44(0)845 230 2102
Email: mail@kcppublications.com
Web site Shop: www.kcppublications.com

Copying notice

Copyright

KCP Publications specialises in publishing educational resources for teachers and students across a wide range of curriculum areas, at both primary and secondary levels.

If you wish to know more about our resources, or if you think your resource ideas have publishing potential, please contact us at the above address.

ANGER MANAGEMENT IN THE PRIMARY CLASSROOM
AN INTERVENTION COURSE FOR 7-12 YEAR OLDS

Contents

Section 1

Why Teach Anger Management?   3

Aims of Programme and Factors that contribute to success   4

An overview of the programme   5

Important ideas about anger   6

Teaching positive behaviour and attitudes   9

Strategies used to bring about behaviour change   12

Using incentives to motivate a child   15

Section 2

The Programme   - Outline of Sessions   17

                   - Session 1   18

                   - Session 2   20

                   - Session 3   22

                   - Session 4   25

                   - Session 5   28

                   - Session 6   30

                   - Session 7   33

                   - Session 8   35

                   - Session 9   37

                   - Session10   40

Follow-up Strategies
                                                                       43

SECTION 1

WHY TEACH ANGER MANAGEMENT?

Positive social behaviour and skills are perhaps the most important skills that children need to learn to lead a successful and happy life. These skills include such things as; conversation skills, turn taking, friendship skills, developing confidence and self esteem, learning adequate self control over emotions and behaviours, being able to consider other points of view, cooperative skills, compromise and problem solving skills, etc. Having these skills not only helps a child to get on well at home and at school but also is likely to lead to a child having more friends, leading a satisfying, productive life and being a much nicer person to know. As children learn these positive behaviours and skills they also tend to develop the positive attitudes and respect towards others that go with these behaviours and skills.

The younger the child the easier it is to teach these skills and conversely the older the child and the more entrenched their antisocial patterns of behaviour the harder it is to teach positive behaviours and attitudes. This is particularly true if the child has been getting what they want through their unacceptable behaviours.

One of the very best things we can do for children is to teach them the positive skills and behaviours they need to get on well in life. We use as much teaching, guidance, reinforcement and discipline as needed to bring this about. If we do this we give children a great start towards leading a satisfying, successful life; If we don't do this then these children are at risk of a whole host of negative outcomes both at school and at home and in later life.

There is a wealth of research showing that children as young as 4 - 6 years of age with antisocial patterns of behaviour and poor self control typically do not grow out of these problems - they just develop into young adults with more serious patterns of antisocial behaviour and anger problems.

What could be more important than doing our very best to overcome these children's behaviour problems and prevent these children from continuing down a destructive path which leads to them damaging their own lives and hurting those around them?

One of the best things you can do for a child is to teach them the social skills, behaviour and self control they need to lead a successful, satisfying life.

This is sometimes very difficult if they have been practising these bad habits for a number of years.

Um. Well maybe I should take some time to teach this. I guess if I don't nobody else will.

And it might just make my retirement a bit more pleasant if I don't have to read about as much domestic violence, abuse murder, bashings, revenge attacks, etc, etc. - most of which are due to people not learning the skills of how to get on with others, problem solving, expressing themselves and managing their anger.

AIMS OF THE PROGRAMME

The aims of this programme are:

- To teach positive social behaviour and skills the child needs to get on well at school and with others.

- To help the child understand and manage their anger in appropriate ways.

- To provide the follow up strategies required to translate the 'head knowledge" the child has gained in the early part of the programme into changed patterns of behaviour in everyday situations.

- To encourage the development of positive attitudes towards others.

Achieving these aims is not an easy task with children whose antisocial behaviour patterns have become quite entrenched and whose antisocial behaviours have been reinforced in the past - but persevere, remain positive and with a bit or luck you will eventually succeed.

Features of The Programme that contribute to success:

1) Increased attention from the teacher in 1:1 or small group situation.

2) A positive friendly relationship with the target child is usually developed.

3) The positive problem solving approach taken - we work to get over problems, we learn from when things go wrong, we can change, we can succeed.

4) Directly teaches children positive social behaviours and why they should engage in these.

5) Reinforces positive behaviours.

6) Incorporates modelling and role plays.

7) Gives the child simple "mental pictures" to help them understand things like anger.

8) Involves an incentive to increase the child's motivation.

9) Raises self esteem of child by providing reinforcement for positive behaviours and by helping them to get on better at school and with others.

10) Follow up strategies including monitoring and feedback to the child regarding their behaviour are built into the programme.

11) Encourages self evaluation.

12) Stresses that each individual is responsible for their own behaviour. We each choose how we behave.

Think carefully about these points and remember them as you go through the programme

(13) An adult actively supporting the child at the end of the programme somewhat like a coach or mentor.

ANGER MANAGEMENT AND SOCIAL SKILLS PROGRAMME - OVERVIEW

- This programme is designed to use with individual children or small groups up to a maximum of 4-6. Although it is all sound material that everyone will benefit from knowing, there is not the same close collaborative relationship built up when used with larger groups or the whole class, as when the programme is used with larger groups. The programme is likely to be most powerful when used with individuals.

- The programme typically runs over ten half hour sessions (usually daily for two weeks) with follow up for the next four weeks or so.

- The preferred option is for the classroom teacher to be released to work through this programme with the child in a 1:1 situation. Alternatively, another teacher with a special interest in this area, or a deputy principal with release time or the principal could run the programme provided that person will ensure that the follow up takes place and that progress is monitored.

- During the withdrawal sessions the child builds up a folder of notes and pictures which are stapled in an A4 folder when the 1:1 sessions end. After going through the folder with the class teacher, then the principal and then the parent the child is given the folder to take home. This builds in repetition of the material covered and will hopefuly lead to these people reinforcing the ideas and strategies learned.

- Each session typically involves discussion, drawing a picture, writing a few main points and sometimes a role play or puppet role play.

- It is important that the teacher running the programme makes a big effort to develop a positive relationship with the child. This is enhanced by being positive, friendly, showing an interest in the child, adopting a helpful problem solving approach and giving lots of encouragement and positive feedback for good behaviours, answers and co-operation. It is also appropriate and necessary to matter of factly confront and discuss any incidents of unacceptable behaviour stating why the behiaviour was unacceptable, the effect it has on others and what a better alternative would be.

- After the two week programme is completed it is essential that the follow up part of the programme takes place to ensure that the "head knowledge" the child has acquired is translated into changed behaviour in everyday situations. The follow-up part of the programme generally consists of:

  ■ The teacher regularly reviewing and reinforcing the ideas and behaviours taught.

  ■ Setting two or three behavioural goals for the child and monitoring these several times per day on a progress chart for two weeks. Then encouraging the child to evaluate their own behaviour on the progress chart for the next two weeks discussing their evaluation at least once a day with the teacher.

  ■ Using any incidents that arise as opportunities to teach and reinforce the positive ideas and strategies covered in the programme.

  ■ Consistently using consequences for unacceptable behaviours including unacceptable. expressions of anger.

IMPORTANT IDEAS ABOUT ANGER

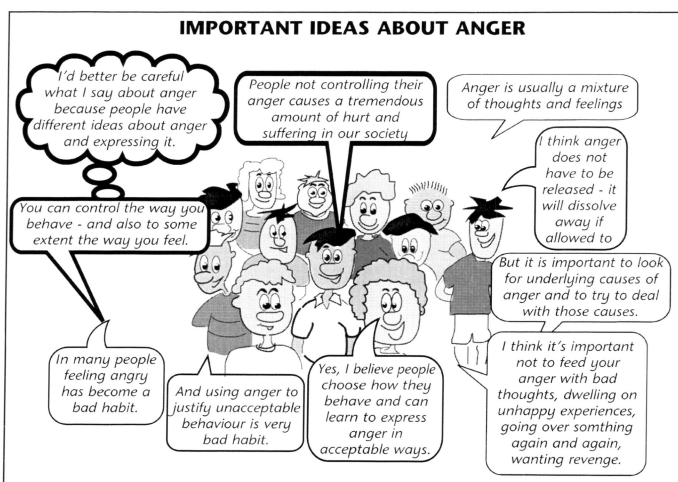

I'd better be careful what I say about anger because people have different ideas about anger and expressing it.

People not controlling their anger causes a tremendous amount of hurt and suffering in our society

Anger is usually a mixture of thoughts and feelings

I think anger does not have to be released - it will dissolve away if allowed to

You can control the way you behave - and also to some extent the way you feel.

But it is important to look for underlying causes of anger and to try to deal with those causes.

In many people feeling angry has become a bad habit.

And using anger to justify unacceptable behaviour is very bad habit.

Yes, I believe people choose how they behave and can learn to express anger in acceptable ways.

I think it's important not to feed your anger with bad thoughts, dwelling on unhappy experiences, going over somthing again and again, wanting revenge.

- It's normal and okay for people to feel angry at times.

- Anger is no excuse for unacceptable behaviour and should not be used to justify it.

- Anger is often a mixture of feelings (emotions) and thoughts.

- Part of feeling angry is physiological - increased heart rate, adrenaline pumped around body, a heightened state of arousal.

- We can all control our behaviour - we each choose how we are going to behave and are responsible for our own behaviour.

- Part of growing up is learning to control one's anger.

- Expressing anger in unacceptable ways often becomes a bad habit.

- Children can learn to express anger in acceptable ways.

- Children often don't grow out of anger problems after the pre-school years - the problem just becomes more serious.

- Children may react with anger to feelings of fear, frustration, anxiety, nervousness, etc, because they haven't learnt (or been taught) to differentiate between these feelings or how to respond to them.

- A child who has learned positive social skills (including managing their anger) is likely to be better adjusted, have more friends and be a happier person than a child who has not.

NORMAL SOCIAL DEVELOPMENT AND ANGER

Feeling angry is a natural human emotion and it is quite common for young children to react with anger to various frustrations including not getting their own way. Some children have quicker temper reactions or more intense anger reactions than others.

Tantrum behaviour from children aged 18 months to 3 years is a common anger response to frustration and can be regarded as normal. However, with consistent management on the part of the parent, children should have grown out of tantrum behaviour by the age of 4 with perhaps just the occasional relapse. The strategies parents are likely to have used to deal with the tantrum behaviour are likely to be some combination of the following:

- Ignoring the tantrum so the child receives no attention for the unacceptable tantrum behaviour
- Not giving in at all to the demands that led to the tantrum behaviour
- Helping children to verbally express their feelings and helping them to deal with their problems and frustrations
- Talking to the child about why they are upset and trying to help the child cope with their feelings - this should be done either before the tantrum begins or after it is over, definitely not during the tantrum
- Recognising when a child is agitated and intervening to prevent a tantrum
- Being a good role model - that is someone who controls their anger and expresses it in acceptable ways
- Teaching children some useful strategies to deal with their anger or upset - eg talking to an adult, going somewhere to cool off, doing some physical activity, counting to ten.
- Consistently using strategies such as ignoring, or a negative consequence such as a timeout, or physical restraint if the child is behaving violently, for unacceptable tantrum behaviour
- Reinforcing positive behaviours particularly examples of when the child has controlled their anger and behaviours that are the opposite of being angry including speaking pleasantly, remaining calm, smiling.

It is vital that the child does not get his/her own way when they have a tantrum.

As children develop mentally and emotionally they are more able to understand anger and emotions, learn to cope with some frustration and learn to control their anger. This is an important part of social development and some children will need more teaching and management than others to learn this self control.

THIS ANGER MANAGEMENT PROGRAMMES INCLUDES:

1.   Discussion With The Child

- what makes you angry?
- what are the consequences of people behaving in an angry way? - hurt, fighting, unhappiness.
- what else could you do when you get angry?
- How do you know when you are getting angry?
- Considering a range of acceptable and unacceptable responses to feeling angry.

Acceptable Responses to Anger	Unacceptable Responses to Anger
Walking away from person making you angry *Cooling off for five minutes* *Thinking about something you like doing* *Telling yourself to "keep calm, stay cool"* *Talking to someone and telling them how you feel*	*Shouting/swearing/abusing* *Hitting/kicking/throwing* *Threatening* *Pushing* *Damaging furniture or buildings*

2. Practising and Reinforcing Acceptable Ways of Dealing With Anger

Get the child to choose (with your guidance) one or two of the acceptable responses to anger and practice them. Praise and encourage the child as they do this.

3. Reinforcing Behaviours the Opposite of Being Angry

The behaviours to encourage are those that are the opposite of being angry and also, dealing with anger in an acceptable way. These include:

> *Smiling, speaking pleasantly, remaining calm, not interfering with/annoying others, dealing with my anger the right way.*

Choose two or three of these behaviours and put them on a tick chart to use with the child.

4. Arranging a Consequence for Unacceptable Expressions of Anger

This could be saying sorry, repairing damage or mess, making up time of outburst in the classroom, missing out on half an hour of play time, etc.

5. Using Angry Outbursts as Opportunities to Teach

When the child has calmed down:
- State the behaviour that was unacceptable or inappropriate.
- Why it was wrong - usually the effect it has on other people.
- That the behaviour prevents him/her getting on with others.
- What would have been a more appropriate thing to do.

Focus on the behaviour and its effect. You can put the above statements in the form of questions to the child. If the child doesn't or won't answer just say the correct answer, perhaps get the child to repeat it and go onto the next question:

Eg: **The Behaviour** - *"What did you do wrong Jamie?"*
The Effect - *"How do you think that made Carl feel?"*
The Alternative - *"What else could you have done?"*

We all have to learn to control our temper as we grow up. If we don't we end up losing our friends and not being happy people.

This teaches the child to think about their behaviour and the effect it has - and what would have been a better behaviour for them to do instead.

TEACHING POSITIVE BEHAVIOURS AND ATTITUDES

The actual teaching of the behaviour involves a combination of the following:

1. **Clearly explaining the behaviour/skill** - often breaking it down into subskills eg, greeting a person could be broken down into the following skills; look at person and make eye contact, smile, say 'hello' in a friendly way, wait for their reply. It can be useful to list these subskills on a chart.

2. **Modelling - the skill should be demonstrated to the child** (it can be effective to use a peer) and it is useful to point out the relevant aspects while the behaviour is demonstrated eg, "See how John made eye contact and smiled".

3. **Supervised practice (includes feedback and reinforcement)** - the child should practice the behaviour while the teacher observes so that the teacher can give praise, encouragement and feedback about whether the child did the behaviour correctly eg, *"That was a good effort John. Remember to look at Jane next time. Let's try it again"*.

4. **Ongoing practice, feedback and reinforcement** - further opportunities for practice must be provided including opportunities for practice in the regular settings eg, class room and playground. Prompting and providing cues can help remind the child to use the skills and when it is appropriate to use them. Peers can be encouraged and/or trained to be part of this process. Using incentives is often necessary to motivate children who otherwise would be unmotivated to learn new skills and to increase the rate of learning.

Positive attitudes that are associated with particular behaviours can be fostered by:

5. **Giving the reasons for doing these behaviours** - as they are explained and demonstrated. eg, "It is good to be kind to people because it makes people feel happy and they are likely to be kind back to you.

6. **Asking the child to verbalise why he/she should behave this way** - it is fine to give the child the answer and then get them to repeat it. This is in effect the strategy of verbal rehearsal. Verbalising an idea or attitude makes the acquisition of that idea or attitude more likely.

7. **Modelling behaviours that reflect positive attitudes.**

8. **Regularly stating positive ideas and attitudes** - and pointing out examples of children doing things that illustrate or reflect these positive attitudes.

9. **Getting the child to engage in positive behaviours that reflect positive attitudes.** Changing behaviour is probably the most powerful way to foster positive attitudes particularly when accompanied by verbalisation of the positive attitude.

Note that with pre-school children, parents (and teachers) teach the positive behaviours that the child needs to learn, and although it is sensible to give reasons and positive attitudes at the same time, the prime focus is on teaching the positive behaviours and the positive attitudes tend to develop along with the behaviour or some time later. In other words behaviours are learned first.

ENSURING THAT BEHAVIOURS LEARNED BECOME A PART OF THE CHILD'S REGULAR BEHAVIOUR PATTERNS

This aspect of teaching behaviours is much more difficult than the first part. Thousands of teachers have taught children social skills only be disappointed that the children with behaviour problems who were the prime focus of the social skills teaching have not changed their behaviour outside the teaching situation.

Ensuring that learned social skills/behaviours become a regular part of the child's behaviour begins with. "Ongoing practice. feedback and reinforcement". Teachers do not stop practising times tables as soon as a child gets them all correct once - rather they continue with regular practice and reinforcement for months knowing that if they do not many children will soon forget them. It is the same with social behaviours. A planned structured programme, reasonably intensive for 24 weeks and then slowly faded, is almost always necessary to get behaviours learned in one setting (eg, small group in classroom) to generalise to another setting (eg, the playground). Some of the following strategies should be incorporated in a structured programme. Generalising skills to the playground will be used as an example.

1) **Behaviours should be practiced in the setting they need to generalise to.** eg, set up a practice session with a group of children in the playground.

2) **Observe the child's behaviour** in the playground so he/she can give the child feedback and reinforcement on whether and how they have used the required skills.

3) **Priming, prompting, providing cues and direct intervention** can be used to make the child more likely to engage in the required behaviours. eg, priming - asking the child what they are going to do in the playground just before interval begins. Peers can be taught to prompt and give guidance.

4) **Use incentives** Check that the incentive is something the child wants. Also, using a class reward where the target child is earning a reward for the whole class can be very positive.

5) **Monitoring progress** - the child's behaviour must be monitored to see whether the required skills/behaviours are being used. eg, the teacher observes for part of lunchtime on the first two days, then checks up using peers after each interval and lunchtime for the next two weeks, then checks up at end of each day, the just checks occasionally provided the skills/behaviour is being used at the required level.

6) **Helping the child see that there are positive results** for the child from using these behaviour/skills. eg, more friends, not in so much trouble.

7) **Combining the above elements in a structural programme** is likely to ensure that the strategies are implemented in a systematic, consistent way. A regular monitored incentive chart can be very effective because it targets behaviours, structures regular feedback and records progress as well as providing an incentive for the child.

INCIDENTAL TEACHING OF BEHAVIOURS

Often the best time to teach a behaviour is when a "natural situation" arises. This may be an example of a child showing a particularly good use of some social skill or an incident where a child has shown a significant lack of appropriate social skills. These should be regarded as opportune teaching moments where there is a certain attention and readiness for learning on the part of the children involved and those nearby. In fact most children learn most of their behaviours through observation and incidental teaching.

Good incidental teaching of behaviours requires the following of a teacher.

- a good knowledge of social skills and how skills often consist of several subskills
- the ability to notice when children engage in appropriate or inappropriate use of social skills
- to give very specific praise, feedback or reprimand that actually tells the child the exact behaviour that was good or not good and to do this frequently and consistently in a mostly positive and natural way
- modelling of appropriate use of social skills
- pointing out the effects of behaviours on others
- verbalising the reasons for using or not using social skills/behaviours
- verbalising the positive attitudes/ideas that go with certain social behaviours

Note that it is often appropriate to use incentives (eg, group points, sticker, public recognition, other reward) **or teaching strategies** (eg, teacher or peer modelling, getting the child the repeat the positive alternative or repeat the behaviour correctly) **or consequences** (eg, apology, write out skill not used, other punishment).

Remember these steps when dealing with negative behaviours:

Step 1 State the BEHAVIOUR - What did the child actually do?
(What did you do wrong Sharon?)

Step 2 State the EFFECT - The positive or negative effective on others
(How do you think that made Carl feel?)

Step 3 State the ALTERNATIVE - What would have been better to do instead?
(What else could you have done instead?)

If the behaviour was negative you can turn the above statements into questions to the child. If the child doesn't or won't answer, just say the correct answer, perhaps get the child to repeat it and go onto the next question. Also it may be appropriate to follow the above steps with an additional teaching strategy or a negative consequence if the behaviour was unacceptable.

By doing the above you are:
- Getting the child to think about their behaviour and the effect it has on others
Hopefully this is fostering empathy and consideration for others also.
- Helping them to see that their behaviour does have consequences.
- Teaching them better alternatives.

STRATEGIES USED TO BRING ABOUT BEHAVIOURAL CHANGE

1)   Going through the material in withdrawal setting:

   - **The child learns through acquiring head knowledge.**

2)   Demonstrating with puppet or person the behaviour or skill the child needs to learn:

   - **The child learns through observing others**

3)   Role plays and practice in the withdrawal setting:

   - **The child learns through practice - but in an artificial setting.**

4)   Priming. prompting, monitoring and feedback about the child's use of the skill or behaviour in the regular classroom or playground setting:

   - **The child learns through practice, repetition and feedback in everyday settings.**

5)   Structuring consistent consequences, positive and negative, depending on the child's use of (or lack of) behaviours and skills taught:

   - **The child learns through the consequences that follow certain behaviours.**

6)   Getting the child to monitor, evaluate and discuss their use of behaviours and skills taught:

   - **The child learns through evaluating and taking responsibility for their own behaviour.**

The more of the above strategies incorporated into the child's programme the greater the learning that is likely to take place. Strategies 4 and 5 are generally necessary to obtain behaviour change in everyday settings and strategy 6 will enhance the likelihood of permanent, long term change.

You know it really would be a good idea to get some information and data on the child"s behaviour before you start

Just look out of the window and you'll get all the data you need - or from his individual file which is bulging with all the incident reports from the last two years.

To make it easy for you there are summary/referral and monitoring forms on pages 12 and 13.

REFERRAL/SUMMARY FORM: ANGER MANAGEMENT PROGRAMME

Referral For Anger

Name _____ Class _____ Date _____

Behaviour causing concern:

1. _____

2. _____

3. _____

4. _____

Skills/Behaviour child needs to learn:

1. _____

2. _____

3. _____

4. _____

Additional Notes: _____

_____

_____

Summary

How has child responded to programme? _____

_____

_____

Changes noted in behaviour: _____

_____

_____

Follow-up strategies used: _____

_____

_____

Positive behaviour changes maintained two months after monitoring stopped: _____

_____

_____

Additional comments: _____

_____

_____

Copiable Page

BEHAVIOUR RECORDING FORM - CLASS TEACHER

Student _____ Room _____ Week of _____ Teacher _____
Behaviour 1 _____ Behaviour 2 _____
Behaviour 3 _____ Behaviour 4 _____

	Monday	Tuesday	Wednesday	Thursday	Friday
Before School					
9.00					
9.30					
10.00					
10.30 **Break**					
11.00					
11.30					
12.00					
12.30 **Lunchtime**					
1.30					
2.00					
2.30					
3.00 **After School**					

This form can provide useful information on a student's behaviour over the course of a week. The teacher notes down whether the child's behaviour has been appropriate (often a tick or dash for each of the target behaviours will be sufficient eg, 1 ✔, 2-, 3-, 4 ✔).
You can record from 1 to 4 behaviours.
Also make a note of any unacceptable behaviour or incidents on the reverse side.

USING INCENTIVES TO GAIN CO-OPERATION AND MOTIVATE THE CHILD

Experience has shown that using an incentive system generally results in the child being more co-operative, positive and motivated to try harder. The child needs to be co-operative and motivated for the programme to succeed. Some children with anger and other behaviour problems may not be keen to discuss their problem behaviour and what they need to do about, it particularly in a group situation. Developing a positive relationship, adopting a helpful problem solving approach and using an incentive system overcome this barrier.

The Behaviour Star opposite has been found to be a practical and effective system with this programme. The star has 33 spots to get coloured in. Each session the child can earn up to four spots coloured in - three for behaviour during the session plus bonus:

1.   Being co-operative.

2.   Speaking pleasantly.

3.   Completing the task.

4.   Bonus - when the class teacher reports something good the child has done in the previous 24 hours or something else that the programme teacher thinks deserves a bonus.

The spots are awarded at the end of each session. The reward is given when all 33 spots have been earned - usually at the end of the 1:1 withdrawal sessions. If a child has not earned all 33 spots by this time they can continue to earn bonus spots for good behaviour until they have all 33 spots.

The reward may be anything that motivates the child - a pencil, ruler, rubber, chocolate bar -whatever motivates that particular child.

NB: The first two target behaviours, being co-operative and speaking pleasantly are key social behaviours to model, teach and reinforce. This is because they reflect positive attitudes and respect towards others and because they are the opposite of antisocial behaviour. A child can't be speaking pleasantly to and co-operative to others at the same time as being angry and behaving in an antisocial way. Therefore one way to tackle anger and antisocial behaviour is to teach, reinforce and increase positive social behaviour.

The idea of dealing with antisocial behaviour by teaching, reinforcing and building up positive social behaviour is an important one.

I like the programme but I don't know about Johnny earning a reward - does he deserve it?

And teaching and reinforcing positive behaviour is something teachers should be good at...
.... shouldn't they?

It might just make it a lot easier and more pleasant for you taking him through the programme... and motivate him and make him more cooperative and...

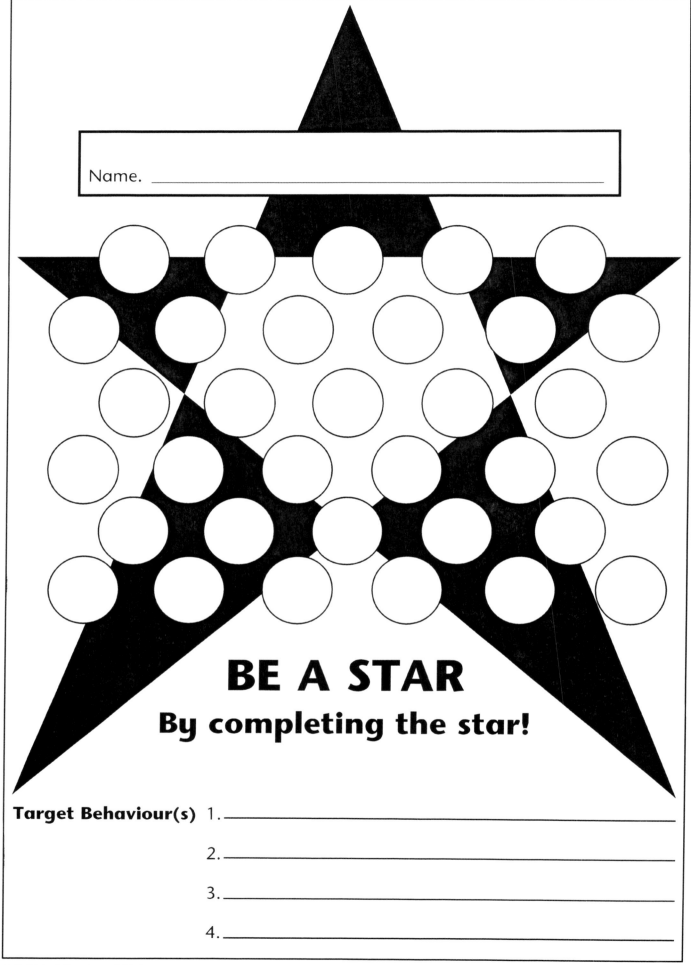

Name. _____

BE A STAR
By completing the star!

Target Behaviour(s) 1._____

2._____

3._____

4._____

16

THE PROGRAMME

Ideally this is ten, half hour sessions over 2 weeks plus monitoring and follow up.

Session 1   "Looking at Me" Chart. Begin to decorate folder. Begin Good Behaviour Star.

Session 2   The Angry Bull and Calm Bull.

Session 3   Prisoner and Happy Person. Good Choices/Dumb Choices.

Session 4   How To Get Over A Problem.

Session 5   How To Be A Good Friend. The Golden Rule.

Session 6   The Anger And Bad Behaviour Fire.
               What Makes You Angry And what Do You Do About It Chart?

Session 7   School Rules. Anger Rules.

Session 8   Warning Signs. Traffic Lights.

Session 9   Anger Train/Processing Your Anger/Who controls you?

Session 10   "I Can Be A Great Person" chart. What Have I learned? Staple folder
               together. Review folder.

- Ensure child has earned reward and organise this.
- Review folder with head teacher, class teacher and parent/s.
- Set goals for "Follow Up Chart" (if parent/s willing could have a chart for home too).
- Continue with Follow Up Programme for 4-8 weeks.

Notes:
- It's okay to carry an activity over to the next session if you have not had time to finish it or to begin the next session's activity if time allows.
- You can fill in spare minutes with completing the folder cover and decorating it.
- Remember to do the Good Behaviour Star at the end of each session and find out about the child's behaviour each day.
- Be positive about the programme and show the child you are interested in them and want them to do well. Point out and reinforce positive behaviours, eg: saying good morning, smiling, speaking pleasantly - and matter of factly deal with any problems that have arisen. Use any behaviour problems as opportunities to teach.

Materials Needed
1. Photocopy off any pictures the child needs from this programme (enlarge the "Looking At Me" chart to A3 size)
2. Some blank sheets of A4 photocopier paper
3. Manila Folder
4. Set of coloured felt pens/crayons.

"LOOKING AT ME"

Objectives:
- To establish a positive relationship with the child
- To get the programme off to a good start
- To find out about the child and their interests

Briefly introduce the programme in a positive way and establish a rapport with the child. State that it is important to learn about how to get on well in life and to overcome problems. Emphasise that the child should enjoy the programme and perhaps introduce the good behaviour star and reward at this point, especially if the child is a bit "anti" about having to do the programme.

Introduce the "Looking At Me" chart (page18 - photocopy to A3 size) telling the child that this gets us started on the programme and helps me to get to know you. You may need to prompt answers about sport, school etc. Often a child won't be able to think of many "nice things about me". Ask questions or give suggestions eg "Well I think you have a great smile", or "Have you got any pets?", "Are you kind to your pet and other animals?" and write down 'I am kind to animals", or "Do you have any jobs to do at home? You may write down the child's answers and just get the child to draw the pictures.

For the "What I Would Like To Be" question you will usually get answers like a nurse, police officer, fireman but then talk about what sort of person they would like to be. With some questioning and prompting get towards the idea that we all want to be happy and friendly and we want other people to like us and write down a sentence covering this. Discuss that this is true for almost everyone in the world - it's part of human nature.

The child should draw pictures in the spaces to illustrate a few of the points written down - or you may take turns drawing the pictures.

Then, after reviewing the positive things discuss that the child also sometimes has problems and gets himself/herself into trouble. Write down anything the child mentions praising any honesty and if the child doesn't mention any, then you mention and write down the problems you are aware of. Discuss that part of growing up is learning to cope with problems, that doing this helps us to get on better with others, and that learning better ways of dealing with problems helps us to be a happier, nicer person. Leave the "Goals I Am Aiming For" box till the end of the programme. The child could put a border around the chart, and if time is available could start decorating the cover of his/her folder. Think of an appropriate title for the folder eg "Learning About Living".

Then go through the target behaviours for the good behaviour star praising the child's good behaviour (if deserved) and being specific about the actual behaviours that earned the spot.The child colours in however many spots they earned. Teacher holds onto folder and papers till end of the programme.

Throughout the programme you should be emphasising, teaching and reinforcing positive behaviours (a bit like coaching) such as speaking pleasantly, using manners, smiling, giving good answers, accepting punishments without fuss, etc, etc.

There should be daily contact with the class teacher (if it is not the class teacher taking the programme) to find out about the child's behaviour. - What positive behaviours the child done that can be reinforced? What might have earned the child a bonus on the Behaviour Star? Any problems that should be discussed? **This is most important!**

"LOOKING AT ME" CHART

Things I am good at

_____
_____
_____
_____
_____

What I would like to be

_____
_____
_____
_____
_____

(name)

Nice things about me

_____
_____
_____
_____

Problems to overcome

_____
_____
_____
_____

Goals I am aiming for

_____
_____
_____
_____
_____

ANGER IS LIKE A WILD BULL

Objectives:
- Have the child understand that anger can quickly lead to accidents and violence

- Realise that anger can hurt innocent people

- Realise that anger can get out of control

Discuss what happens at a rodeo. Some cowboys try to ride wild bulls. What might happen when they do? Get hurt, stomped on, gored etc. If the bull is angry the cowboy is likely to get hurt. Get the child to draw (or colour in if using the next page) a wild bull bucking off a cowboy with the cowboy flying through the air towards the ground.

Discuss: The wild bull is a bit like anger and bad behaviour (label the bull). when anger and bad behaviour are out of control (like the wild bull) then other people often get hurt and upset. Write this beneath the picture of the wild bull: "Anger and bad behaviour - when it is out of control people get hurt and upset."

Get the child to draw (or colour in) the picture of the bull being led by a ring through its nose (child draws in ring and rope). Discuss that just like when the bull is under control when we control our anger and bad behaviour no one gets hurt or upset. Write this beneath the bull being led: "Anger and behaviour - under control - no problem!" If time allows, you can begin the next session or child can work on his/her folder.

Complete the Behaviour Star.

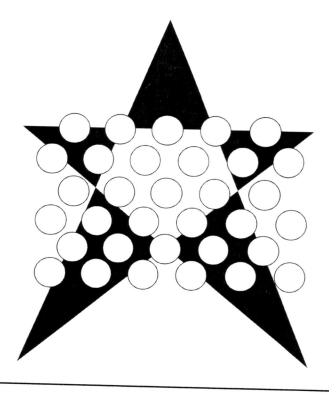

_____

_____

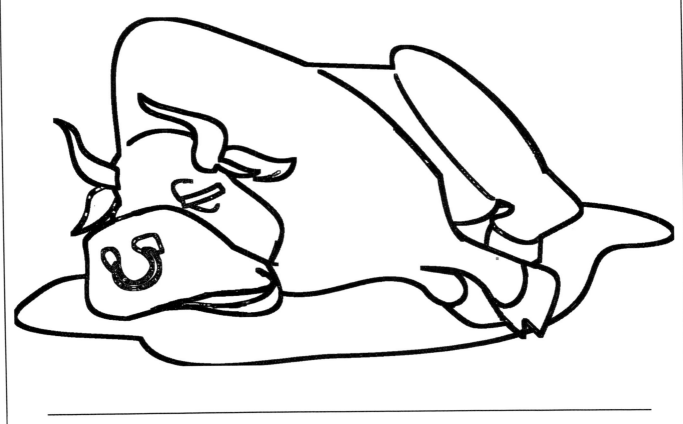

_____

ANGER MAKES YOU A PRISONER

1. Get the child to join the dots and make the picture of a prisoner with a ball and chain attached to his/her leg. Discuss; why is this person not free? Do you think they are happy? Write beside the picture,
    "Prisoner - not happy - not free".

2. Discuss: If you have an anger problem or other behaviour problem then you are like the prisoner and the ball and chain represent the behaviour problem. Label the ball, *"behaviour problem"* or *"anger problem"* and underneath add *"stops us being the great person we could be".*
    Discuss: The anger/behaviour problem interferes with you getting on well with others, doing well at school and being happy.

3. Get the child to draw a picture of a happy person (eg, skateboarding, trampolining, jumping around) with a big smile. Discuss: this person is happy and free because they don't have any anger/behaviour problem. Write this beside the picture *"Happy and Free - the way we are meant to be".*

"How To Make Good Choices"

4. Get child to draw a small picture of him/herself on the left side of a blank page half way down.
    Discuss: We all choose how we behave. We make lots of choices everyday, (eg whether to try hard at our work, who to play with, what to wear, etc. etc). Often we don't even think much about the choices we make because how we behave has often become a habit. when we make choices we can either make good choices that help us, dumb choices that don't help us and often get us into trouble.

5. Draw two diagonal lines from the person - one going up to a heading "Good Choices". Get the child to give two examples of good choices at school and two examples of good choices at home. Discuss why these are good choices and write them down under the heading. Do the same for Dumb Choices and write the examples down.

6. Go through the chart "How To Make Good Choices" (p24) with the child discussing each point and illustration. Emphasise that we need to think about the consequences of the choices we make have both for ourselves and for others.
    Beneath the child's picture write this "We each choose how we behave and are responsible for what we do".

Finally discuss one or two further examples with the child and ask them what "good choices" they are going to make today. Complete the Behaviour Star.

_____

_____

HOW TO ...MAKE GOOD CHOICES

We all make choices about how we behave everyday.
As we grow older we must learn to make good choices -
choices that help us get on well with others and
choices that are right for ourselves too.

Now lets see, what are the different choices I can make?...

Good Choices ▸ What might happen?

Dumb Choices ▸ What might happen?

1. Think

- What can I do?
- What are the different choices I can make?

Come and join us. We're going to cause some trouble

Hey

2. Think again

- About each choice and what will happen if I make that choice.
- What are the consequences or results of each choice likely to be?

More thinking! Making good choices sure involves a lot of thinking

3. Decide which choice is best

- Is the right thing to do?
- Doesn't hurt or upset other people
- Keeps you out of trouble

I'll just walk away and take no notice of them

4. Do it

And if it's a good choice tell yourself "Well done, I made a good choice"

Ha Ha

Look

BABY

5. Make good choices a habit

I've just dumped my bad habit of making dumb choices.

*Making dumb choices...
...didn't help me
...didn't make me happy
...and didn't solve any problems
...it just made me unhappy and got me into trouble.*

Copiable Page

HOW TO GET OVER A PROBLEM

Look at the "How To Get Over A Problem" Chart on page 26.

Discuss: When we have a problem it's a bit like a train that's gone off the rails. What do you need to do when a train has derailed? Put it back on the rails so it can carry on. When we have a problem we need to get over the problem and make a fresh start - we need to put our train back on the rails. Discuss the steps to go through.

Some difficult children will realise to say sorry (step 4). it's no use getting stuck at this point. You should model an appropriate apology and get them to repeat it. If they refuse to apologise you can say something like *"part of growing up is learning to say sorry. If you can't say sorry this time I hope you will learn to soon"*, and go onto Step 5. You have still modelled an appropriate apology and let the child know that is the right thing to do?
Anytime they do apologise or accept a punishment without fuss then praise these behaviours because both are positive social skills to encourage and reinforce.

Also discuss that often part of getting over a problem is accepting a punishment without fuss. Spend time discussing this. Is the child able to? How do they feel about it? Are they big enough (or tough enough) to take a reasonable punishment without fuss?

Look at the Worksheet on p27.

Get the child to copy down the five main points shown on page 26.
Add "There are 5 steps to getting back on the rails" in the speech bubble.

Perhaps discuss a few of the child's recent problems and how these could have been overcome using these steps eg, *"How could you have cooled down? Where could you have gone to do this? who could you have talked to? Should you have said sorry? What will you try to do next time?*

Complete Behaviour Star.

HOW TO ...GET OVER A PROBLEM

Such as anger, fighting, being unkind

There's been a problem, things went wrong and I've ended up off the rails. I need to sort out the problem, get back on the rails and make a fresh start.

Whoops! I've got to get back onto the rails

1. Cool off

I may need to leave the room or sit quietly by myself for a while.

*I need to get calm first...
... and then think.*

2. Think

Either about something I like doing to help me cool off or about the problem and how it can be solved.

*That's OK!
Thats what friends are for.*

3. Talk to someone

The head teacher, teacher or a friend.

Thanks for listening to me and helping me to sort out the problem.

4. Say Sorry

If you did something wrong and if you feel able to... otherwise go to Step 5.

Great! I am back on the rails again. Away I go!

5. Make a fresh start

Take a deep breath and start again.

*Well Done!
You have got over your problem.*

FULL STEAM AHEAD!

Copiable Page

BACK ON THE RAILS

PUTTING THE TRAIN BACK ON THE RAILS
HOW TO ...GET OVER A PROBLEM

1. _____

2. _____

3. _____

4. _____

5. _____

27

HOW TO BE A
GOOD FRIEND

Get the child to brainstorm ideas about what it means to be a good friend.
What does a good friend do? You may prompt ideas by questioning.
List down the child's answers. Then compare and discuss the child's list with
the points on the "How To Be A Good Friend" chart (p. 29).

Head up a sheet of paper "How To Be A Good Friend" and get the child to copy down the main
points and illustrate a few of the points eg, a smiley face for point 1, a little figure with a
speech bubble saying something positive for point 2, and some children kicking a ball for point 6.

When this is done ask the child about their best friend and go through the points giving a tick
for each of the points that the friend does. How good a friend are they? Then do the same for
the child. Help them to be honest. Any things they can do to be a better friend?

Ask the child it they know the Golden Rule of friendship and if they know it is nearly 2000 years
old. Tell them if they don't know.

"Treat other people the way you would like them to treat you"

Discuss this rule and what it means. Think of examples. If everyone followed this rule people
would get on much better and be happier.

Head up a sheet of paper ~The Golden Rule". Get the child to draw a person and a large
speech bubble. Write the Golden Rule in the speech bubble and suggest that the child asks their
teacher and their parent if they know the Golden Rule.

Complete Behaviour Star.

HOW TO ...BE A GOOD FRIEND

It is very important to be able to make friends and to know how to be a good friend. Everyone likes to have friends and havind friends helps us to feel happy - And when you've got friends you can have lots of fun with them.

This is a nice car you've got Edward.

You can come and play with me if you like

1. Smile at people

2. Say nice things to your friends

3. Ask them to join in games

Well you see .... and....... and....... and....... and....... and.......

I've sure got a lot of listening to do.

4. Listen to your friends when they talk to you

5. Think about how your friend feels

- be kind and show you care about them

I fell over and hurt my knee.

Come on, I'll go to the sick room with you.

6. Play and have fun with your friends

And remember the golden rule. Treat other people the way you would like them to treat you.

"To have a friend you need to be a friend"

THE ANGER AND BAD BEHAVIOUR FIRE

1.   Duplicate the worksheet on page 31.
     Cut out the drawing of the log fire, the logs and the fire extinguishers.

2.   Issue a sheet of blank paper. The child writes the title "The Anger and Bad Behaviour Fire"

3.   Discuss: How could you build up the fire and make it burn more? Answer - Put more logs on.

4.   How could you make the fire smaller or put it out?
     Answer - use a fire extinguisher.

     Anger and bad behaviour is like a fire - we can make our anger and bad behaviour worse or we can cool down our anger and bad behaviour.

5.   Paste six or seven logs on one side of the page and six or seven fire extinguishers on the other side. Discuss and write inside the logs the things that make the child's anger, behaviour or the problem worse eg. swearing and shouting, hitting and fighting, calling names and abuse, wanting revenge, thinking bad thoughts. refusing to cool down.

6.   Discuss and write inside the extinguishers the things the child could do to cool down and get over the problem - eg. walking away, talking to someone, ignoring teasing, going somewhere to cool down, talking to yourself, just forgetting about it. Discuss which of the ideas in the buckets the child thinks would be best for them to do.

What Makes You Angry Chart

Fill in a copy of the "What Makes You Angry" Chart with the child. See the sample on page 32. You may need to prompt answers and make sure tile real problem behaviours the child has get listed in the column "what Do You Do?"

Then mark each of these with a red felt pen discussing whether they are a good choice or dumb choice and why.

Then list some better alternatives and why these are good choices. Put a tick beside the ones that the child thinks are best for them to try and do. (This chart repeats some of the material on the previous page).

Complete Behaviour Star.

THE ANGER AND BAD BEHAVIOUR FIRE

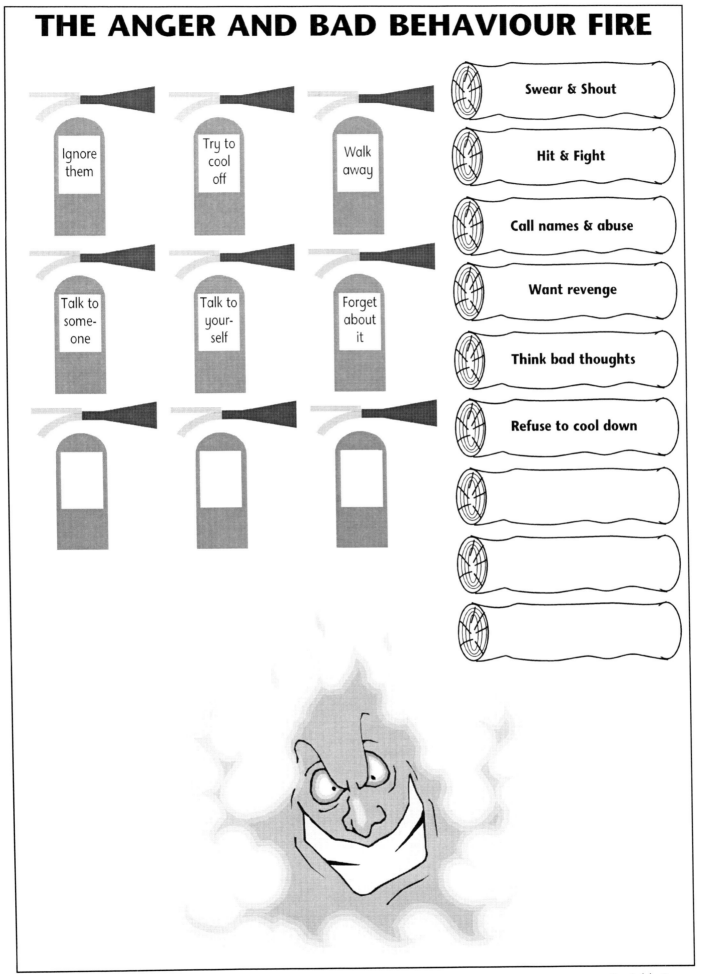

WHAT MAKES ME ANGRY

WHAT MAKES ME ANGRY

WHAT I DO WHEN ANGRY

WHAT I COULD DO INSTEAD

ANGER RULES

In general children referred for this course don't get on that well at school they often have trouble following school rules and conforming to reasonable standards of behaviour. Therefore it is worthwhile spending some time discussing why there have to be school rules, why they need to be followed and getting the child's agreement that they should try to follow these rules.

A. After a brief discussion about rules at school get the child to suggest some rules and list them down. You may prompt the child by saying we need at least one rule for each of the following:
- getting on well with the teacher
- getting on well with others
- getting on with our work

Discuss and compare the child's list with chart on page 34. "How To Get On Well At School". Head up a sheet of paper "How To Get On Well At School" and get the child to copy down the main points.

Optional - you may photocopy the School Rules Chart, fill in the rules and get the child to sign. Following these rules could earn a child a bonus on their Behaviour Star:

SCHOOL RULES

1. _____
2. _____
3. _____
4. _____
5. _____

Following these rules will help me get on well at school. If I do these things I can be pleased with myself and the teacher will be pleased with me too. I will try to do these things: Signature: _____ Date: _____

B. Then discuss that there are also rules for dealing with anger. Ask the child - what are the things they should do/shouldn't do. Discuss and copy the following rules.

THE ANGER RULES

It's okay to feel angry but...

DON'T:
- Hit or hurt
- Swear at or abuse others
- Throw things or damage property

Do:
- Talk to someone (about how you feel and why you are angry)

HOW TO ...GET ON WELL AT SCHOOL

It is important that we all get along well at school so that we can learn what we need to, get on with each other and be happy. For the school to be a pleasant place we all need to follow these rules.

It's great to see all these happy smiling faces

1. Do what the teacher asks straight away

The teacher can't run the class properly unless everyone does this.

I really like the way everyone stopped and listerned straight away

2. Speak pleasantly to others

This sets a pleasant tone and make everyone feel happy and srcure.

Jill, can I please borrow your rubber.

Yes Jane you can

3. Co-operate with each other and be friendly

So we can work together and be happy.

Can I please join your game.

Yes, Our game will be better with 3 people

4. Try hard at our work

So we can learn as much as we can.

Well done Sam. You can be really proud of your work.

This work is good fun when I try hard. It is doing my best that is important

5. Leave other people and their belongings alone

"A successful society depends on children learning the above"

Our class is a great place to be when we all follow the rules

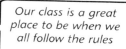

Warning Signs and Physiological Reactions

A. Discuss what happens to your body when you get angry. (How much detail you go into will vary with the age of the child. Also children may feel anger in different ways). In general when people get angry adrenaline is released into the blood stream and pumped around the body, heart rate increases, and people may sweat, go red in the face, feel a knot in their stomach, clench their fists or teeth, start to scowl etc. It is the body's way of getting ready for action and very similar to the "fear" reaction. The body is getting ready for fight or flight. As well our brain interprets what is happening eg, when someone knocks into us our brain may think *"it was an accident, I don't need to worry or get angry"* Or *"they knocked into me on purpose. They had no right to. I am entitled to get angry"*.

Discuss with the child what happens in their body when they get angry eg. clench fists, sweat, breathe fast, go red in the face. List these on the chart on page 36. Discuss how they feel and what they are thinking when they start to get angry.

Discuss whether there are any particular "triggers" particular events, situations or people) - they may well be little things that often trigger the child's anger. Getting the child to think about and discuss the last few dines they got angry can help identify their physical reactions, feelings, thoughts and triggers.

B. Discuss that being able to recognise when we are getting angry can help us manage our anger. Say "What we really need is a set of traffic lights for our anger". Discuss what the traffic light colours mean.

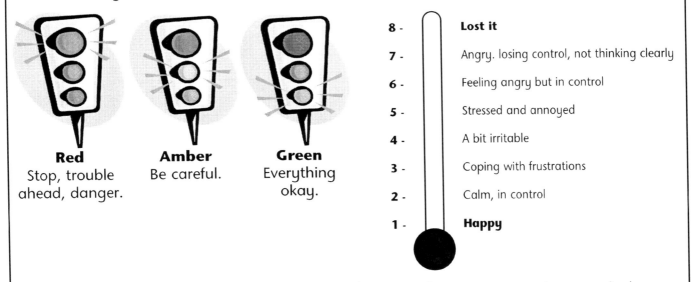

Red
Stop, trouble ahead, danger.

Amber
Be careful.

Green
Everything okay.

8 - **Lost it**

7 - Angry. losing control, not thinking clearly

6 - Feeling angry but in control

5 - Stressed and annoyed

4 - A bit irritable

3 - Coping with frustrations

2 - Calm, in control

1 - **Happy**

These ideas can also be covered using the idea of a meter that measures a steam engine's pressure. The engine explodes when the pressure gets into the purple zone.

- Discuss and compare with the chart from page 36 just completed.
- How does the child know what colour zone they are in?
- What might their thoughts and feelings be in each zone?
- How might their body be acting?

Complete Behaviour Star

MY WARNING SIGNS OF ANGER

	Feelings or Thoughts	Trigger or Event	My Body's Reaction	What I Did	Outcome
1.					
2.					
3.					
4.					

PROCESSING YOUR ANGER

Discuss that part of growing up is learning to control your anger and deal with it. You don't have to ignore it - you can process it. Discuss the following steps using examples of when the child has felt angry write these down on a sheet of paper.

Steps in Processing My Anger (using your brain to sort out the problem)

Step1
Do I need to cool down?

Step 2
Am I feeling angry (or sad, upset, embarrassed, anxious, frustrated, frightened. confused, nervous, jealous)? Discuss what situations could lead to these different feelings.

Step 3
What is making me angry? (Need to identify the reason).

Step 4
How can I deal with this problem? (Think of ways to deal with it).

Step 5
Do I need to talk to someone?

Step 6
What would be a good choice to make now?

Step 7
What do I need to do now?

What are two things I can do to help me process my anger better?

1. _____

2. _____

A child is likely to need an adult to help them work through these steps. These could get photocopied onto card and go inside the child's desk, or inside a book cover, or on the wall.

WHO CONTROLS YOU?

Get the child to colour in the picture of the person hunched over by the "temper devil" on his back on p.39. Draw in a speech bubble "I want to be in control". Write "Don't give away your power and self control to your temper" by the side.

Get the child to colour in the person with the small pack. Libel the pack "Temper Under Control" and fill in the speech bubble "I am in control of me. I can control my temper. That makes me powerful".

Discuss the idea of a person having power and that part of that power is having self control. By allowing others and the things they do to make you angry (push your buttons) you are giving away some of your power and self control. Write down "Part of growing up is learning to control your temper".

Get the child to colour in the person at the bottom of the page. In the left speech bubble write "keep your cool - don't lose it". Then in the space provided write "doing these things can help me keep my cool and feel positive". List 4 or 5 of these.

eg
- smiling
- speaking pleasantly
- acting friendly
- being cooperative

Complete the Behaviour Star.

GREAT PERSON CHART
GOAL SETTING
ANGER QUIZ

A. **Fill in the "I can be a great person chart"** P.41 with the child. Perhaps colour the lines with a bright felt pen and get the child to put theft name in the middle. Ask the child questions similar to the following and fill in all the spaces. (This goes on the inside front cover of the manila folder:

eg. What is your favourite food?
What is something you are good at? What is your best subject at school?
What is one nice thing about you?
What are three things you have learned doing this programme?
What is one thing you are trying to achieve?
Do you know the golden rule?
etc. etc,

You can add in your own positive comments as well as prompt answers. When you have finished write in the rectangle at the bottom "I can be a great person - if I make up my mind to be one ". Discuss this.

B. **Staple folder together.**

The "Looking At Me" chart (page 19) is stapled to the back cover of the manila folder. ALL the pages are put inside the folder.

The Behaviour Star is stapled to the inside flap of the folder so you see it as soon as you open the folder. Draw a figure on the front cover with two speech bubbles. In one write "Be A Winner! - Keep your cool and don't make dumb choices". In the other write "I can be a winner - but only if I try".

Complete the "Goals I Am Aiming For" box on the "Looking At Me" chart. Discuss what the most important goals are with the child's teacher first - so that you can guide the discussion with the child to ensure.practical, important and realistic goals are set. Two or three of these goals are then put on the child's daily monitoring chart.

C. **Review Folder** - go through the folder page by page briefly reviewing what has been covered in the programme.

D. **Anger Quiz**

Go through the anger quiz with the child. Discuss answers as necessary. You will need to refer to some of the diagrams as you go through the quiz.

I CAN BE A GREAT PERSON

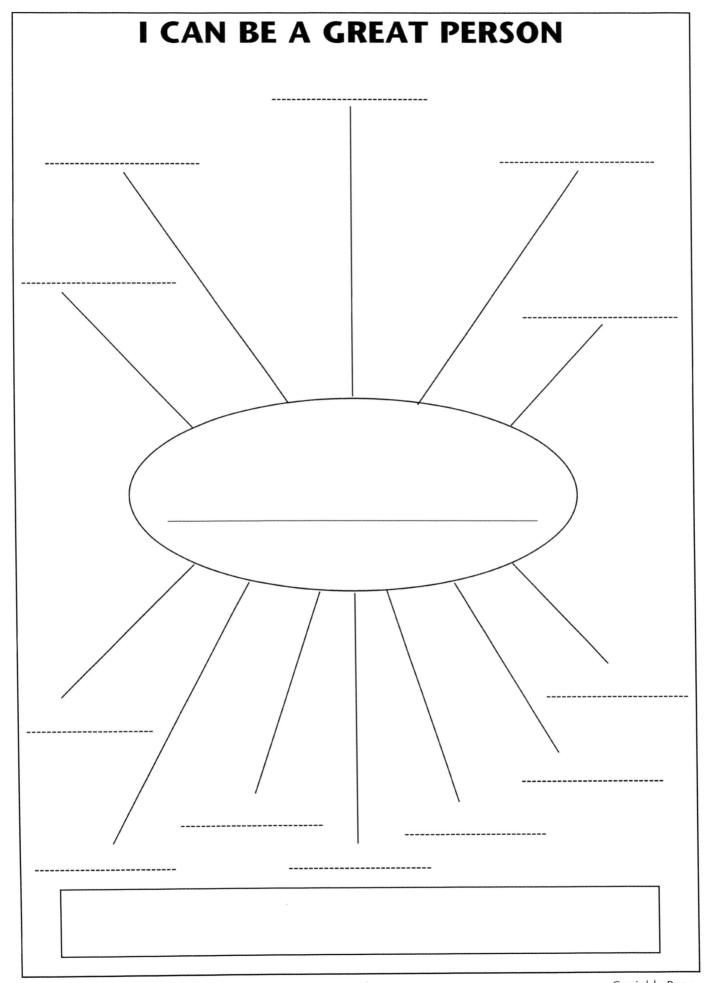

ANGER QUIZ

1.   What is the wild bull like? *(Anger and bad behaviour out of control)*

2.   What is the bull being led by a ring through its nose like? *(Anger and behaviour under control)*.

3.   What is the way we are meant to be? *(happy and free)*.

4.   What is the ball and chain like on the prisoner? *(a behaviour/anger problem)*.

5.   What are the types of choices you can make? *(good choices and dumb choices)*

6.   Who chooses how you behave? *(I do)*

7.   Who is responsible for your behaviour? *(I am)*

8.   Why do we use the picture of the train off the rails? *(because it is like when you have a problem or get into trouble you go off the rails)*.

9.   What do you need to do when you go off the rails?
     (get over the problem, make a fresh start)

10. How many of the five steps for getting over a problem can you remember? *(cool off, think, talk to someone, say sorry, fresh start)*.

11. What are three things a good friend does? *(smile, say nice things, listen, asks you to join games, thinks about your feelings, plays with you)*

12. Can you remember the "Golden Rule"? *(treat other people the way you would like them to treat you)*

13. What is the fire like? *(anger and bad behaviour)*

14. What are two logs that make the anger and bad behaviour fire worse? *(eg, swearing, hitting, wanting revenge, refusing to cool of)*

15. What are three things you can do to cool off the anger fire? *(eg, cool off, walk away. talk to someone, ignore, forget about it)*

16. What are you going to try and do when you get angry? *(eg. Talk to someone)*.

17. Read the anger rules to me?

18. Why is the person hunched over? *(temper wants control)*

19. Why do I need to keep control of my temper? *(eg. so I don't get into trouble, or hurt or upset others, it stops me being happy, people won't like me)*

20. What are the goals on my chart?

21. How will achieving these help me?

One tick for each correct answer or part of answer.

FOLLOW-UP STRATEGIES

DON'T STOP HERE
- *The programme is not finished yet. Don't stop when you are half way to success*

The programme is not finished yet! If you do stop here it is quite likely that the child's everyday behaviour in the classroom and playground will not change. You have given the child "head knowledge" but that will not usually translate into permanently changed patterns of behaviour without continued reinforement, revision and systematic follow-up. The next few pages give strategies and suggestions for how to turn this "head knowledge" into changed behaviour in everyday situations.

This programme up to this point should have:
- given the child knowledge and strategies
- established a positive relationship
- provided motivation and impetus for change
- improved the child's behaviour through extra 1:1 attention, daily contact and support from you.

The following strategies are designed to maintain the positive change and hopefully lead to these positive changes becoming permanently changed patterns of behaviour.

Follow-up Strategies:

1. **Revision and reinforcement of material learned**
   - reviewing folder with class teacher, principal and parents
   - teachers/parents regularly referring to the ideas/skills covered and using some of the language, eg good choices/dumb choices.

2. **Start and consistently use the "Going For Gold' Chart** to monitor the child's behaviour giving the child clear, specific feedback as you do so. (p 44)

3. **Consistently dealing with and using consequences for unacceptable behaviour.**

4. **Maintaining a positive relationship with the child and acting as an encourager, coach, mentor, motivator and problem solver.**

GOING FOR GOLD

Name _____

Week of: _____

Going for Gold Goals	Monday	Tuesday	Wednesday	Thursday	Friday

Cleary specify required behaviours as goals. You could divide days into morning and afternoon. You may use rewards to motivate the child to achieve targets set. e.g., for each target you achieve you earn 2 minutes on the computer. You might also use a punishment for targets not achieved, e.g., 5 minutes staying in at lunchtime for each target not achieved.

STRATEGY 1: REGULAR REVISION AND REINFORCEMENT OF MATERIAL

After completing the programme it should be reviewed with the class teacher, the principal and parent/s. This not only involves repetition for the child but also familiarises the teacher, principal and parent/s with the material so that they can reinforce the ideas and strategies the child has learned by:

- reminding the child of the ideas and strategies learned
- reinforcing the positive behaviours covered in the programme
- revising the material covered if things have gone wrong encouraging and motivating the child to keep trying
- using the language and ideas when discussing the child's behaviour, eg *"You've gone off the rails. What do you need to do to get back on the rails?" "Was that a good choice or a dumb choice?" "You made a great job of staying on the rails." "Remember your goals, keeping your cool and speaking pleasantly."*

STRATEGY 2: "GOING FOR GOLD" MONITORING CHART

It is essential to follow-up the sessions with this monitoring chart for 4-8 weeks.

There should be two or three goals set for the child. It is a good idea to involve the child in setting these goals but discuss with the class teacher which behaviours are most important for the child and try to incorporate these in the goals (children are often receptive to suggestions for goals at the end of the programme - or choose one each). Suitable goals could be:

- Keeping my cool
- Speaking pleasantly
- Discussing problems with the teacher
- Not annoying or interfering with others
- Playing co-operatively
- Not answering back or arguing

These goals should be monitored and the chart marked 2-3 times per day with the child present so that clear specific feedback about the child's behaviour can be given. Positive reinforcement is given for positive behaviours and problem behaviours can also be dealt with by discussing what behaviour was unacceptable, the reason for it and, what a better alternative would have been. Use a punishment if appropriate.

The child receives a tick for each goal achieved and a dash if they have not achieved the goal. You may wish to use an incentive, eg every tick earned equals one minute computer time or free time with a friend.) Reduce monitoring the chart to once or twice a day after 2-3 weeks. Then after 3-4 weeks the child can mark the chart themselves and take it up to the teacher at the end of each day. This self-monitoring encourages the child to take responsibility for theft own behaviour. After the child has successfuly self-monitored for 2-3 weeks try a week without the chart. Keep up the level of positive verbal feedback when you phase out the chart. At any stage the child can be placed back on the chart or moved to more frequent monitoring if the child's behaviour starts to deteriorate.

STRATEGY 3: CONSISTENT USE OF CONSEQUENCES FOR UNACCEPTABLE BEHAVIOUR

Part of changing difficult children's behaviour is consistently providing consequences they don't like when they engage in unacceptable behaviour. During the 10 Sessions you will have repeatedly clarified with the child which positive social behaviour is expected, which behaviour is unacceptable and that behaviour choices the child makes have consequences. Now is the time for the child to consistently find out that choosing unacceptable behaviour (including not controlling their anger) has negative consequences.

Appropriate consequences could include.

- verbal or written apology
- restitution or compensation of some sort, if appropriate
- copy rules or fill in incident report
- stay in at interval, lunchtime or after school
- miss out on some enjoyable activity or privilege
- isolated from group
- making up time of anger outburst

In general, the child should be informed of the unacceptable behaviour and the consequence in a calm but firm manner. It may be appropriate to discuss the behaviour and what led up to it but the focus should be kept on the child's unacceptable behaviour and this should not be allowed to be excused or minimised.

The child should know what sorts of punishments are likely to follow unacceptable behaviours so that he/she can predict the likely consequences of their actions.

Some children have not learned to accept punishments without making a big fuss about it (or learned that making a big fuss sometimes results in not having to do their punishment). For such children the following strategies can be useful:

1. Ensure the child knows which punishments are likely to follow certain behaviours.
2. Explain and practice the punishment (eg leaving the room) when the child is calm.
3. Reducing the punishment by up to half if the child does the punishment without fuss or doubling the punishment if the child makes a fuss.
4. Praise the child for accepting the punishment without fuss, eg *"That was good the way you just sat quietly for five minutes without any fuss"*.

Reasonably short punishments used consistently are generally sufficient, and it is good if they can be related to the misdeed in some way.

STRATEGY 4: MAINTAINING A POSITIVE RELATIONSHIP WITH THE CHILD

A positive relationship with a difficult child can overcome a lot of problems. With older, tougher students who are prepared to face any consequences you can use and throw them back in your face - whether you can establish a positive relationship with the child or not will often determine whether you succeed or fail with that child. A positive relationship will often make the difference between whether a student is "anti" and unco-operative or friendly and willing to co-operate.